THE
BRIGHTON & HOVE

INDEPENDENT CAFÉ GUIDE

A.J. EVANS & L.V. PRICE

Vespertine
Press

First published in the UK by Vespertine Press 2010

Copyright © Vespertine Press 2010
Text © A.J. Evans & L.V. Price
Photography © L.V. Price, Eleonora d'Ambrosio & James Dean White

A catalogue record of this book is available from the British Library

ISBN 978-0-9566582-0-3

Cover & layout design by L.V. Price

Printed & bound in the UK by Four Corners Print

Printed on 9 Lives Offset - paper manufactured from 100% recycled fibre

FSC

Recycled
Supporting responsible use
of forest resources
www.fsc.org Cert no. SA-COC-001654-BT
© 1996 forest Stewardship Council

CONTENTS

Tab Key

W   Wireless Internet   **O**   Outside Seating

V   Vegetarian Food   **D**   Disabled Access

(Please note - Disabled access may not include access to toilet facilities.)

INTRODUCTION

For millions of people around the world, the morning would be incomplete without coffee. Whether prepared at home in a cafetière, sipped at a café table whilst reading the paper or rushed from a take-away cup on the way to work, the much needed caffeine pick-me-up provides a welcome interlude in our daily routine. But over time, not content with its mere stimulating effect, our appreciation for coffee becomes more refined. The aroma, the nuances of flavour and the skill behind its preparation begin to take precedent over the simple purpose of kick-starting our day. It is then that we begin to actively seek out places that can live up to our growing expectations - where every cup far exceeds the weak and bitter stimulant we had for so long accepted, though never loved. At this point it is impossible to go back; the coffee house and café become a part of our everyday lives.

Most people have their own idea of what makes a great café. Some are used primarily as work places while there are others whose well situated pavement terraces provide spectator seats for the passing human cabaret. Then there are the lively meeting spots where discussion drowns out the sounds of the espresso machine and a theory or debate is being expounded at every table. Indeed, ever since the first coffee houses opened in London in the mid-seventeenth century, they became renowned as hotbeds of political discussion as well as trading posts that would go on to spawn institutions like the London Stock Exchange. By the eighteenth century coffee houses were dubbed *penny universities* - so called because, for the entrance fee of a penny, one had access not only to coffee but to the education afforded by newspapers, pamphlets, discussion and gossip. Conversely, throughout history there have always been cafés purposely frequented by the solitary coffee drinkers, those hideaways for people who, as Viennese satirist and café enthusiast Arthur Polgar says, *"want to be alone but need companionship to do so."*

Whilst the criteria for a great café still has much to do with its situation and ambience, today the merits of its coffee matters more than ever before. Since the advent of the first *Gaggia* espresso machines in the 1940s, the general standard of coffee and espresso based drinks has risen. Coffee is now often regarded as a speciality foodstuff much like wine and is diligently sampled and produced with the same expert attention. Nowadays, becoming a barista is a career choice rather than just a part-time job and the role of the master taster, who cups and grades coffee on its aromas, flavours, tastes and 'mouthfeel', has become increasingly prevalent. The popularity and appeal of the World Barista Championship, held in London for the first time this year, has also grown extraordinarily since its inception in 2000.

The coffee movement today - sometimes referred to as the Third Wave of Coffee - focuses on improving every stage of coffee production, with an insistence on using only speciality grade Arabica beans, promoting single origin coffees from around the world and achieving perfection in latte art. There is also a greater emphasis placed on employing Direct Trade principles when sourcing coffee beans, a system of trading that cuts out both the middle men and the organisations who have the ability to control certification. This approach helps the coffee suppliers to deal more closely with the farmers themselves, building mutually beneficial relationships, addressing social and environmental concerns and paying them a price relative to the quality of the coffee they produce. One of the earliest roasters to follow these principles in the UK was London's Monmouth Coffee, though the trend has been established for some time in nations such as Australia and America, where they have enjoyed a more evolved coffee drinking culture. Unfortunately it has taken far longer for the British to relax their allegiance to the greasy spoons and tea rooms, where the standard of coffee is generally low. But whilst it is still seen as a nation developing its coffee drinking habits, in London and the South East - where 75% of our yearly espresso is consumed - speciality coffee roasters and high end cafés have flourished in recent years.

The city of Brighton and Hove has long since possessed all the ingredients necessary for a thriving café culture. The vibrant street markets and shopping areas, its abundance of bars and restaurants whose tables spill over onto the pavements, as well as the eccentric characters, street performers and musicians that fill the city's streets, all go towards the creation of a cosmopolitan and care-free atmosphere. The diverse mix of residents and visitors, a thriving arts scene and its reputation for welcoming a largely liberal, bohemian crowd also contribute to the cafés' popularity here. Now, with the help of café owners and virtuoso baristas from historically strong coffee cultures, as well as the growing diversity of the London scene, the city's profile for high standards of independent cafés and their coffee is finally living up to its other well renowned virtues.

Even a city like Brighton and Hove, which prides itself on its autonomy and support of local trade, is suffering the effects of recession and of multinational companies squeezing the life from smaller independents. Supporting local businesses is therefore more pertinent than ever. We hope that you will frequent and enjoy the independent cafés of Brighton and Hove as much as we do and that in some small way, this book will help showcase and promote the excellence of these and other local businesses throughout the city.

NORTH LAINE

Though there is much debate as to its official origins, the term *laine* is thought to be derived from an Anglo Saxon expression meaning smallholding or strip of land and bears no relation to the word *lane*. In the mid-nineteenth century the area was largely populated by saw-mills and foundries, and home to Brighton's largest slum, but in the last thirty years the North Laine has blossomed into a vibrant, bohemian area regarded by many to be the heart of the city. Some of Brighton's most famous cultural attractions, such as the Royal Pavilion, the Brighton Dome and the Theatre Royal are located within the North Laine. Today, the North Laine is also renowned for its array of second hand and vintage clothes boutiques, specialist book and record shops and its high number of restaurants, bars and largely independent cafés. The laid back bustle of the area is especially enjoyable on the weekends when the Saturday market stalls are set out on Upper Gardner Street and the area is crowded with shoppers and day-trippers making their way to the seafront.

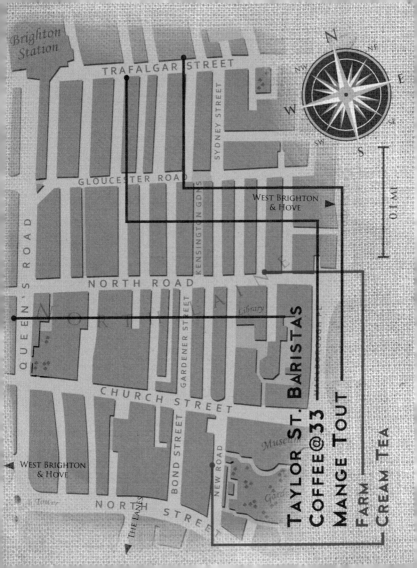

TAYLOR ST. BARISTAS

28 QUEENS ROAD
BRIGHTON, BN1 3XA
T: 07886 199 706
www.taylor-st.com

According to the famous proverb, *necessity is the mother of invention.* It was precisely this notion that led to the creation of Taylor St. Baristas; the brainchild of three Aussie siblings responding to the low standards of coffee on offer in the UK. That the idea arose during a bleak English mid-winter may have led the trio to yearn more acutely for their homeland, though ultimately it wasn't the sunshine that they wished to import to Brighton - it was the coffee.

Four years after their move to the South coast, Taylor St., named after the road in Sydney where the owners once lived, has remained true to the purpose of its conception. Having outgrown its former base within the confines of the Travelbag shop, the café moved to a much larger site along Queen's Road, near Brighton station. In correspondence with their relocation, Taylor St. has broadened its range of Australian café food to include toasted homemade banana bread, ricotta pancakes and Bircher muesli, along with an extended variety of snacks and sandwiches.

However, striving for coffee perfection is still the main focus at Taylor St. In collaboration with Union Hand-Roasted, their bespoke Rogue espresso blend is designed to promote the diversity and seasonality of coffees from around the world. Throughout the year, as different crops arrive at the roastery, the blend is changed to incorporate and showcase distinctive coffees that are balanced accordingly for variants of flavour. As such, the coffee here is a constant work in progress with the aim of creating a blend for espresso and espresso based drinks, like the flat white or cappuccino, that is sweet, complex and rounded.

Currently the blend is composed of beans from the Lambari Farm in Minas Gerais, Brazil, from Costa Rica Finca San Jeronimo and from Ethiopian Sidamo, which adds floral notes and gives a more complex aroma. To ensure that the hard work they put into creating the perfect coffee blend delivers the best possible results, Taylor St.'s baristas are trained in coffee, tea and chocolate theory, equipment use and maintenance, espresso theory and practice, milk texturing and art, alternative brewing methods - such as aero press and pour-over - and tea brewing. Bearing in mind such effort, it's no wonder that Taylor St. are at the vanguard of Brighton's growing coffee scene.

COFFEE@33

33 TRAFALGAR STREET
BRIGHTON, BN1 4ED

———◆———

Perhaps the greatest charm of a good independent café is its ability to retain the original seeds of spirit that inspired it, without compromising the fundamental elements of quality and service it set out to achieve. Without the need to mass produce or to bow down to corporate influence, an independent can nurture the more important elements that go into creating an atmosphere and a standard that its customers can really savour.

A stone's throw from Brighton station, down the busy thoroughfare that is Trafalgar Street, Coffee@33 takes these ideals and pushes them that little bit further. In 2008 the site, which once housed Café Abroad, was stripped back to get to the bare boards and white walls that its new owners sought. The proprietors - a Ukrainian barista and an Italian chef - wanted no distraction from the coffee and food that they ardently create and prepare on site. To this day the décor remains minimal: clean lines, hand-made wooden benches and the coffee sacks used as cushions on the much coveted window seats, all allude in style to the high-end cafés of London.

Using a Monmouth blend of three South American beans, the result is a medium to dark roast with a very smooth finish, equally as good as an espresso or with milk; a combination that is often afforded the 'best in Brighton' tag by reviewers on the many online message boards. The Brazilian beans constitute the majority of the blend, bringing sweetness and caramel flavours, the Colombian beans add smoothness with notes of fruit and almond and the Guatemalan element creates a chocolatey finish. Coffee@33 also source all their milk through local Sussex farmers.

Not to be overshadowed, the food is entirely homemade, right down to the lovingly baked focaccia bread. Along with sandwiches and paninis, there are also flapjacks and brownies on offer, and if you're feeling inspired, they create cookie dough for you to take away and bake at home.

That cafés like Coffee@33 exist in Brighton is testament to how small scale businesses with the right amount of expertise, zeal and dedication can flourish. This is a place that has been created by coffee and food lovers, *for* coffee and food lovers. In an industry where similar ideals can be overshadowed by the money-driven spectre of big business, Coffee@33 remains happy to be exactly where it is, sticking to what they set out to do in the first place. The beauty of that, like all the best things in life, lies in its simplicity.

MANGE TOUT

**81 TRAFALGAR STREET
BRIGHTON. BNI 4EB
T: 01273 607 270**

———————◆———————

In France it is said that a bistro can become the essence of the neighbourhood in which it dwells, where the routine of its daily life keeps time with the rhythms of its locale. From the early morning coffee, to the lunchtime rush, the afternoon lull and the early evening meal, the café remains a steadfast observer of the passing hours.

On the North side of Trafalgar Street, Mange Tout has more of this relaxed café-bistro feel than most in Brighton, maintaining that traditional Gallic flair for food and drink within a fresh and modern environment. The interior is bright and airy and the south facing windows shed plenty of light onto the morning papers. The blackboard menu wall, the photographic work of local artists and the mixture of modernist and traditional seating all add touches of interest to the surroundings. As a statement of intent, the espresso machine takes pride of place in the café so that the customer can observe a trained barista preparing their coffee, made with Small Batch sourced beans and served the French way - with a glass of water and a miniature meringue.

The terrace of tables and chairs outside is ideal for those who prefer drinking their coffee whilst taking in the passing charms of the avant-garde North Laine crowd. Wherever you decide to position yourself, the food is simple and honest and prepared by highly skilled chefs using wild, organic and free-range produce sourced from local farms and suppliers. The main menu largely consists of French favourites such as moules-frites and, of course, escargot. The tartines and Eggs Benedict, with freshly made Hollandaise sauce, are considered their unofficial speciality and the homemade cakes and pastries are definitely worthy of any self-respecting French kitchen.

Opened in March 2009, the café has already gained a healthy local following. On the weekends, when the North Laine really springs to life, those conversant with Mange Tout's menu flock to sample the fine food, the irrepressible charm of its French owners and the laid back sounds of FIP radio that meander through the café. The union of tradition and modernity infuse Mange Tout with its own unique atmosphere, bringing a contemporary impression of the continental café experience to Brighton. *Vive la France!*

FARM

99 NORTH ROAD
BRIGHTON, BN1 1YE
T: 01273 623 143
www.farmsussex.co.uk

Opened in late 2009, Farm is owned and run by a group of local farmers, who grow the vegetables, rear the livestock and produce the dairy products that are used in making the café's homemade meals and sandwiches. This ensures that each of these ingredients have been locally and mindfully produced, that everything has been ethically farmed, is as fresh as possible and remains seasonal throughout the year. Where certain foodstuffs need to be acquired from elsewhere, Farm prides itself in using bread from Ockham's Lighthouse Bakery and coffee from Borough Market's renowned Monmouth Company, who themselves work closely with coffee farmers around the world to make certain that the quality, sustainability and emphasis on fair and equal trade is upheld.

Inside the café, which is positioned next door to the famous Bill's Produce Store, the feel is unsurprisingly reminiscent of a farmhouse kitchen with the church pews, distressed furniture and milk cans used as stools making the interior a homely, informal place in which to relax. Their farmers market, recently opened further up North Road, will bring yet another slice of the Sussex countryside to the North Laine.

CREAM TEA

13 NEW ROAD
BRIGHTON, BNI IUF
T: 01273 325 112

A s café locations in Brighton go, Cream Tea has a vantage point that is hard to beat. From a seat on their pavement terrace opposite the Pavilion Gardens one can take in the historic charms of Brighton's cultural quarter as well as the sights and sounds of New Road's eclectic street performers and musicians.

Behind its curved glass frontage the café is bright and modern, though with touches of the traditional tea room to which the name refers. The display cabinet at the counter is well stocked with homemade cakes, scones and pastries, with an ice cream machine providing welcome refreshment during the heat of the summer. Along with the customary English Breakfast and Earl Grey tea on offer, the café also serves a selection of loose leaf teas by the renowned Tea Pigs company. Whilst tea rooms are ordinarily not well known for the merits of their coffee, Cream Tea has enlisted the expertise of Small Batch to make sure that their coffee is not only locally sourced and freshly roasted, but also that the standards are up there with the quality of the view.

EAST BRIGHTON
&
KEMPTOWN

Kemptown is named after Thomas Read Kemp who formulated the plans for the original Kemp Town estate in the early nineteenth century, creating large and elegant homes for the affluent social elite. Though the one-word title Kemptown now refers to a much larger area, the regency style architecture that is perhaps most notable in the magnificent Sussex Square and Lewes Crescent, still upholds the air of grandeur attributed to the original designs. As a whole, Kemptown is rejuvenated having gained a less than positive reputation in recent years for its generally run down appearance. Today the area is rich in character derived from the originality of its artisan and creative residents, whilst it is also home to a large proportion of Brighton's gay community. Further to the East, the Bristol Estate, Whitehawk and the Craven Hill Estate, are often collectively referred to as East Brighton, whilst to the North and West of Kemptown lies the tranquillity of Queen's Park.

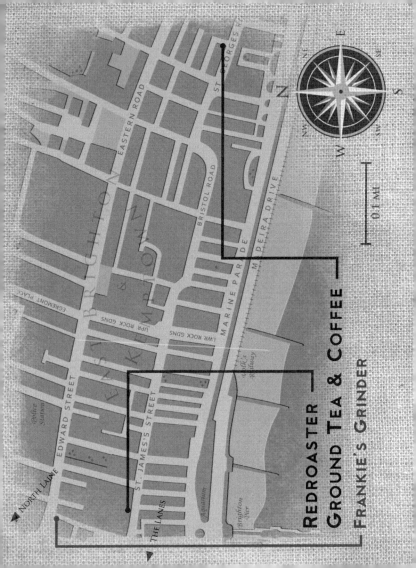

REDROASTER
GROUND TEA & COFFEE
FRANKIE'S GRINDER

0.1 Mi

REDROASTER COFFEE HOUSE

ID ST. JAMES'S STREET
BRIGHTON, BN2 IRE
T: 01273 686 668
www.redroaster.co.uk

I n the decade since Redroaster established itself on St. James's Street, it has become something of a Brighton institution. From its windows, the views of the locality have changed and shifted with the times. The vicinity, once called Little Laine was, even up until several years ago, an area in the midst of slow decline, gaining undesirable monikers that were a far cry from its reputation in the nineteenth century as the Bond Street of Brighton. But whilst the aspect has altered, Redroaster has maintained its immutable appeal, taking root as an integral part of the reinvigorated St. James's street community.

As you would expect from the area, the café attracts a diverse cross-section of visitors which creates a lively, communal atmosphere. Underneath the skylights set into its high ceilings, the sounds of chatter and the aroma of roasted coffee waft throughout the spacious room. The antique coffee grinders on the ledge opposite the counter allude to the home roasting experimentation the café owner undertook when the business was in its fledgling years.

That was during the late eighties and early nineties speciality coffee boom in North America, where US companies were preparing to branch into the European market. It was on this wave of interest that the seeds of Redroaster's influence were sewn in Brighton, setting up shop on the corner of Meeting House Lane and Ship Street in the Lanes. Today, Redroaster has branched out and now run their own separate roastery on Arundel Mews in Kemptown. Here their experts cup, roast and distribute bespoke blends for some of the most established venues in Brighton including Komedia and the Infinity Foods Café. Their head roaster, Paul Stephens, also won the UK Cup Tasting competition held by the Speciality Coffee Association of Europe in 2010.

With its origins so firmly embedded in the creation of fine coffee, it is no wonder that Redroaster's produce has gained such a reputation. As well as boasting an extensive range of single origin coffees from Ethiopia, Peru, India, Brazil and Guatemala, all roasted on site using their eponymous red roaster, they also serve sandwiches, flapjacks, pastries and cakes. In the evenings the café becomes home to one-off music events, poetry readings, book launches and even tango lessons.

With the high turnover of independent cafés in the city, Redroaster's ten year tenure deserves kudos. So whilst sitting under the café's canopy, watching the bustle of St. James's street pass you by, it is worth being reminded that times change but quality endures.

GROUND
TEA & COFFEE

36 ST. GEORGES ROAD
BRIGHTON, BN2 IED
T: 01273 696 441

———————◦———————

Hard work and attention to detail should never be afterthoughts when running a business, something that those at Ground Tea & Coffee know all about. Before collaborating, the owners cut their teeth working long hours in restaurants, gaining all the expertise they required to branch out on their own. At the cafés conception the design and fitting was undertaken almost entirely by themselves, making the project a labour of love from the very beginning. It means that from the cork insulated ceilings to the custom-made shelving, every detail of the décor has been dutifully overseen and considered.

As a continuation of their commitment, Ground adhere to direct trade principles when sourcing their coffee, working in collaboration with Union Hand-Roasted to make their own blend that combines beans from Guatemalan and Brazilian farms. The Guatemalan beans bring honey, red fruit, dark chocolate and butterscotch flavours whilst the Brazilian beans make for a sweet and rounded cup with tones of almond and cocoa.

The estate in Brazil that produces this coffee - owned by the Rebetez Mariani family - places consistently in the national 'Cup of Excellence' competition and is considered a model farm for its commitment to its workers and their families. At Ground the coffee is then made to order with shots pulled for 25 seconds on a La Marzocco espresso machine. Along with their own blend, they also have rotating, single estate guest coffees from around the world including Ethiopia, Mexico, Rwanda and El Salvador, which are prepared using a separate grinder. As the name suggests, Ground Tea & Coffee also serves a fine selection of 12 loose leaf Jing teas, served in glass, single cup teapots.

The café itself is small but perfectly formed and its south-east facing windows fill the space with light, making for an ambience that changes throughout the days and months. There is also an emphasis on seasonality with the rotation of coffees, teas, jams and pastries. To round things off, the book shelf provides an extensive range of good quality reading material to enjoy over your coffee.

To some, the details that go into achieving coffee perfection may seem complex, but in fact the message at Ground is simple: if it's not as good as it can be, why bother? It is no accident then, that the results of their endeavours are of such high quality.

FRANKIE'S GRINDER

180 EDWARD STREET
BRIGHTON, BN2 0JB
T: 01273 818 888

F or the past seven years, Frankie Vaughn's on Edward Street has been lauded by locals as one of the prime lunch spots in Brighton. With a choice range of bespoke sandwiches, bagels and salads, all freshly prepared using mainly local ingredients, perhaps the only attribute missing was a place to sit and enjoy a cup of coffee. But then, in late 2009 Frankie Vaughn's owner set up a boutique coffee bar in the more spacious corner plot next door and kitted it out with a La Marzocco espresso machine, a counter decorated with hessian coffee sacks and all the renowned food options previously confined to their deli. Thus, Frankie's Grinder was born.

To ensure that their coffee lives up to the high standards set by their food, they have designed Little Frankie's Blend with Hove-based coffee roasters Small Batch, which they also sell ready ground to be enjoyed in the comfort of your own home. And if you need your coffee to go, the service hatch that gives onto Prince's Street makes for a speedy return to the office. Lunch breaks have never been so well catered for.

THE LANES

The Lanes, also referred to as the South Lanes, are the heart of the old fishing town of Brighthelmstone. Much of its layout is derived from the paths, or 'twitterns', that once ran between allotments and gardens in the centre of this 14th century dwelling. Today the Lanes are commonly taken to be bounded by the Old Steine to the east and the seafront to the south, along with North Street and West Street - two of the four streets that were marked on the earliest existing map of Brighton. The area is well known as the city's historic centre and is largely populated by antiques and jewellery shops, fashion boutiques, traditional English pubs, restaurants and cafes. Due to their proximity to the seafront, the Lanes are often full of activity, making it the perfect place to window-shop as you meander to the beach. Despite the modernisation of a large proportion of buildings during the 18th and 19th century, the narrow twist of alleyways continue to exude the atmosphere of a medieval town with a number of 400 year-old cottages remaining, as well as the Cricketers, which is claimed to be Brighton's oldest pub.

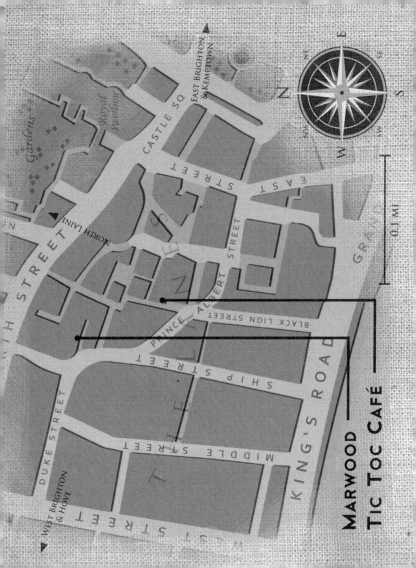

MARWOOD
TIC TOC CAFÉ

MARWOOD

52 SHIP STREET
BRIGHTON, BN1 1AF
T: 01273 382 063

———————◆———————

E ver since the first European coffee house opened in Venice in 1645, great writers, artists and thinkers have used them as unofficial workplaces and meeting spots. Whilst some cafés have become infamous because of their creative inhabitants - think the Café de Flore or Les Deux Magots in Paris, where Sartre and Simone de Beauvoir founded their existentialist theories - Brighton has never had such a place. That is, perhaps, until now.

Since opening in late 2009, Marwood has rapidly built its reputation amongst the city's large creative community as a place to convene and to work. The very reason Marwood came to fruition was reliant on the work of many such minded people, not just its owners, who all chipped in with their own goods, ideas and services to create a kind of hybrid space of many influences. It is no wonder then that its wonderfully cluttered interior also houses the sense of a community-shared project and is imbued with no small amount of humour.

Mannequins adorn the walls alongside framed toy animals and pictures of Tommy Cooper and Oliver Reed, whilst the tables are made from salvaged doors and arranged in such a way that sharing is almost customary, a conscious decision to aid the meeting of new people. New additions to the scenery seem to appear overnight so that the café is forever in a state of eccentric flux. A washing line pegged with business cards and flyers hangs the length of the counter, behind which skilled baristas diligently create coffees that look almost too good to drink. Though the food menu is limited to snacks like Breville toasties and homemade cakes, the focus on the quality of coffee is enough to warrant a lengthy stay on its own.

The café's upper stories accommodate Marwood Studios, which is home to design offices, desk shares and a Mac specialist. It is also where their free, in-house *Arty* magazine is produced, which aims to showcase local artists, photographers, galleries and social spaces. Amid the jumble of the café walls downstairs, the work of some of the magazine's contributors is also exhibited.

Whilst it may be some time before the café becomes famous for any of its clientele, Marwood is nonetheless attracting interest for all the right reasons. As with everything else here, the only rule appears to be that there aren't any... and somehow it seems to be working.

TIC TOC CAFÉ

53 MEETING HOUSE LANE
BRIGHTON, BN1 1HB
T: 01273 770 115
www.tictoc-cafe.co.uk

The Lanes of the twenty-first century are densely populated by antiques shops, boutiques and jewellers, but they still retain much of their historical charm. Tucked in the bustling heart of these 'twitterns', housed within a listed building on Meeting House Lane, Tic Toc Café is an ideal place to stop and charge up on caffeine and calories.

The nucleus of the café's design is derived from the coffee shops of Amsterdam, the green of the exterior, for example, being one of only eight shades of colour permitted within the city's famous Jordaan District. But stepping inside it becomes clear that, in both its produce and its décor, Tic Toc draws inspiration from right across Europe. Rustic French signs decorate the walls, there is a selection of fine English teas and there is also something distinctly European about borrowing one of the café's blankets and sitting on the small terrace with a cup of Belgian hot chocolate in the winter months.

All this is juxtaposed with sixties-inspired clocks, quirky floral wallpaper, toy ornaments and dashes of historical detail and the mish-mash of antique furniture and feature walls make the interior a space in which one notices a new facet on every visit. The food at Tic Toc is a continuum of its decorative mélange with traditional British snacks like Welsh rarebit and bacon butties given a continental twist. The lunchtime speciality here is the open sandwich, with a large selection of delicious fillings and served with healthy side salads.

As with any good cafe the quality of its coffee is paramount, a consideration that Tic Toc's owners addressed early on. Before opening they teamed up with the Small Batch Coffee Company and worked alongside them to create a blend of coffee specific to their own design. The result: a rich taste, sweetened ever so slightly by the addition of 4% Indian beans, a combination that goes some way to affirming the cheeky sign outside that reads, *Probablement the best coffee in Brighton*. Certainly, as a place to enjoy some time out, there is no doubt that Tic Toc is one of the city's best.

Probablement the best Coffee in Brighton

TIC TOC
CAFÉ

OPEN DAILY

TEL:
01273 770115

www.tictoc-cafe.co.uk

TIC TOC
CAFÉ

OPEN DAILY

TEL:
01273 770115

www.tictoc-cafe.co.uk

WEST BRIGHTON
&
HOVE

It is said that whereas Hove was built, Brighton grew. It grew until the boundary between them was blurred and until the two combined to form one city. As you head west from Brighton's centre the change occurs gradually with narrow streets and fisherman's houses morphing into the regency splendour of Brunswick Square and Adelaide Crescent, their boulevards lined with trees and parkland. Hove has undoubtedly retained its identity as an independent town with thriving shopping areas and a cultural input that both rivals and complements its larger neighbour.

The western seafront is a many varied strip with old fisherman's arches turned into everything from galleries to nightclubs. The skeleton of the West Pier has changed from derelict eyesore to creative inspiration and the pétanque pitches and Hove's lawns provide both a refuge and a recreation ground. There is certainly much to savour and enjoy in this part of Brighton... and Hove, actually.

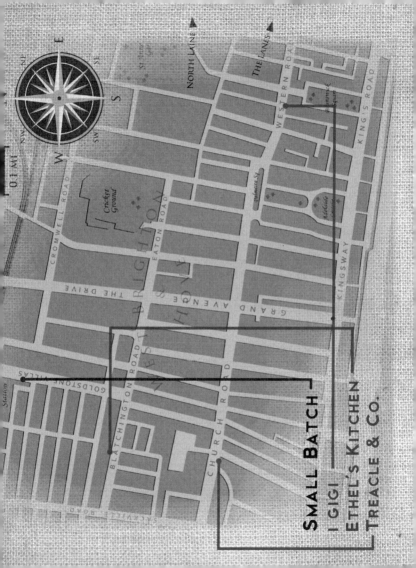

SMALL BATCH
I GIGI
ETHEL'S KITCHEN
TREACLE & CO.

SMALL BATCH COFFEE COMPANY

68 GOLDSTONE VILLAS
HOVE, BN3 3RU
T: 01273 220 246
www.smallbatchcoffee.co.uk

Small Batch Coffee Company was established in 2008 with the focus of filling a gap in the UK market for the type of small, family run roasteries that have long since been commonplace in New Zealand and Australia. In the years that have elapsed Small Batch has flourished, becoming one of the main coffee suppliers to the pubs, bars, restaurants and independent cafés of Brighton and Hove.

Their roastery near Hove station incorporates a high-end espresso bar, serving coffee produced from the finest quality Arabica beans that are roasted daily in batches no bigger than 12kg to ensure freshness. Their espresso blend is changed throughout the year in order that it remains seasonal and incorporates the best of the current crops from around the world. Being an independent coffee roasting company also allows Small Batch to work alongside café owners to produce bespoke blends depending on their individual requirements and to provide barista training where it is required.

Like many of the best boutique roasters and coffee shops, Small Batch adhere to a direct trade principle that not only ensures the highest quality product but also serves the ethical purpose of rewarding the farmers and growers fairly for the speciality grade coffee they produce. In turn, this method also allows the supplier to work directly with the coffee farmers to ensure that social, environmental and wildlife conservation issues meet or exceed local requirements. From a customer point of view, whether buying wholesale or a single cup at the café, it gives assurance that their purchase is of the highest standard.

On a weekday the aroma of the freshly roasted coffee beans drifts from the Small Batch doorway, a sign that the coffee you're drinking will have been roasted, tasted and hand blended a matter of hours before it reaches your cup. From the very beginnings of the growing process, through to the beans that are ground in the bars and cafés across the city, Small Batch will have considered all the elements that go into producing the perfect cup of coffee. Proof, if any were needed, that small, bespoke roasteries like this are having a big impact on the way we think about coffee throughout the UK.

I GIGI CAFÉ

31a WESTERN ROAD
HOVE, BN3 1AF
T: 01273 775 257
www.igigigeneralstore.com

One of the many simple pleasures to be had in Brighton & Hove is finding the cafés that are tucked away or hidden from view, those places that are stumbled upon and end up exceeding all expectations.

Housed on the first floor of their General Store, the beautifully presented i gigi café most definitely falls into this category. The antique spiral staircase on the ground floor leads up into the bright one room kitchen-café where the rustic furniture is bathed in light from the expansive, single-paned front window that overlooks the bustle of Western Road. The space is tastefully decorated in shades of cream and white and the understated elegance of the space makes for a relaxed atmosphere. The food on offer at i gigi is as homely and wholesome as the décor, and their lunch boards, Welsh rarebit and delicious homemade cakes - displayed beneath traditional bell jar cake stands - are famed amongst those in the know. i gigi also serves Brazilian blend Monmouth coffee and a selection of Tea Pigs whole leaf teas making it a perfect spot for breakfast, brunch, lunch, or just a well deserved caffeine break. It's all just waiting to be discovered.

ETHEL'S KITCHEN

**59 BLATCHINGTON ROAD
HOVE, BN3 3YJ
T: 01273 203 204
www.ethelskitchen.co.uk**

Named after Grandma Ethel, whose granddaughter owns and manages the café, Ethel's Kitchen merges the essence of her culinary legacy with modern British food, loose leaf teas and speciality grade coffee. Upon entering you are greeted by a fine display of homemade cakes, and the bone china cups and saucers on shelves behind the counter are a nod to the wholesome traditions of afternoon tea. From the front room of Ethel's Kitchen a small flight of stairs lead down to another seating area where the exposed floorboards, antique furniture and display dishes adorning the walls are a continuum of the relaxed, rustic decoration throughout the café.

Their coffee is sourced by Union Hand-Roasted who apply a similar diligence to producing high quality, ethical coffee as Ethel's Kitchen do in realising the spirit of British home cooking. On the menu, staple favourites like eggy bread, homemade soups, jacket potatoes and traditional Sunday roasts are given a modern twist, with every meal made from scratch using mostly organic produce. In short, it's all healthy, hearty, homely fare. Grandma would be proud.

TREACLE & CO.

164 CHURCH ROAD
HOVE, BN3 2DL
T: 01273 933 695
www.treacleandco.co.uk

With a decade of experience as a pâtisserie chef behind her, Melody Razak established Treacle & Co. in 2007 with a view to supplying her wares to the sweet toothed inhabitants of Brighton & Hove. Her selection of handmade cakes, biscuits and brownies are made the old fashioned way with only the best local, free range and organic ingredients. Working within the confines of her home kitchen, the business grew to the point where the space, and indeed her neighbours, could no longer cope with the increasing burden of the late night baking sessions and the popularity of her finished creations. Thankfully, in July 2010, the Treacle & Co. HQ was relocated to a much more convenient home on Church Road, complete with original 1930s era tiling. Along with all the home-baked delicacies for which the company is renowned, the café also serves up Monmouth Coffee Company's organic espresso blend and tea courtesy of Kemptown's Metrodeco. Throw into the mix a selection of vintage school chairs and tables, a window display featuring genuine Canadian moose antlers and a jumble of antique mirrors and home wares and you have the quirkiest new café in town.

BRIGHTO

OVERV

Hove
Station
•

Brighton
Station
•

NORT

PA

WEST BRIGHTON
&
HOVE

PAGE 58

•
Shopping
Centre

THE

PA

•
West
Pier

N & HOVE
N MAP

LAINE

2

● Royal
Pavilion

EAST BRIGHTON
&
KEMPTOWN

PAGE 32

NES

6

Brighton
● Pier

THE
BEST OF THE REST

Other independent cafés worth visiting in Brighton & Hove

NORTH LAINE

COCOA

48 Queen's Road
Brighton, BN1 3XB
T: 01273 777 412
www.cocoabrighton.co.uk

NIA

87-88 Trafalgar Street
Brighton, BN1 4ER
T: 01273 671 371
www.nia-brighton.co.uk

MOKSHA CAFFÈ

4-5 York Place
Brighton, BN1 4GU
T: 01273 248 890
www.mokshacaffe.com

ROCK OLA

29 Tidy Street
Brighton, BN1 4EL
T: 01273 673 744

SEASONS CAFÉ

36 Gloucester Road
Brighton, BN1 4AQ
T: 01273 689 388
www.seasonscafe.co.uk

INSIDE OUT CAFÉ

95 Gloucester Road
Brighton, BN1 4AP
T: 01273 692 912

THE DUMB WAITER

28 Sydney Street
Brighton, BN1 4EP
T: 01273 602 526

OFF BEAT COFFEE BAR

37 Sydney Street
Brighton, BN1 4EP
T: 01273 604 206

KENSINGTON CAFÉ

1 Kensington Gardens
Brighton, BN1 4AL
T: 01273 570 963

BRIGHTON COFFEE CO.

35 Kensington Gardens
Brighton, BN1 4AL
T: 01273 690 643
www.brightoncoffee.co.uk

IYDEA

17 Kensington Gardens
Brighton, BN1 4AL
T: 01273 667 992
web.mac.com/iydea

CAFÉ DELICE

40 Kensington Gardens
Brighton, BN1 4AL
T: 01273 622 519
www.cafedelice.co.uk

INFINITY FOODS CAFÉ

50 Gardner Street
Brighton, BN1 1UN
T: 01273 670 743
www.infinityfoods.co.uk

TEMPTATION
56 Gardner Street
Brighton, BN1 1UN
T: 01273 673 045
www.brightontemptation.com

CAPERS
27 Gardner Street
Brighton, BN1 1UP
T: 01273 675 550
www.capers-brighton.com

CAFFÈ ITALIANO
24 New Road
Brighton, BN1 1UF
T: 01273 687 753

PAVILION GARDENS CAFÉ
Royal Pavilion Gardens
Brighton, BN1 1UG
T: 01273 730 712
www.paviliongardenscafe.co.uk

REDWOOD COFFEE HOUSE
97-99 Trafalgar Street
Brighton, BN1 4ER
www.redwoodcoffeehouse.com

EAST BRIGHTON & KEMPTOWN

TEA COSY
3 George Street
Brighton, BN2 1RH
www.theteacosy.co.uk

METRODECO & MDTEA
38 Upper St. James's Street
Brighton, BN2 1JN
T: 07956 978 115
www.metro-deco.com

THE BOOKROOM CAFÉ
91 St. George's Road
Brighton, BN2 1EE
T: 01273 682 110
www.kemptownbookshop.co.uk

THE KEMPTOWN TRADING POST & COFFEE SHOP
28 St. George's Road
Brighton, BN2 1ED
T: 01273 698 873
www.kemptowntradingpost.co.uk

SPINELLI COFFEE

24 Garnet House
College Road
Brighton, BN2 1JB
T: 01273 818 819

111 St. James's Street
Brighton, BN2 1TH
T: 01273 818 084
www.spinellicoffee.co.uk

HOME

Egremont Place
Brighton, BN2 0GA
T: 01273 674 456
www.homebrighton.co.uk

THE LANES

NAKED TEA & COFFEE COMPANY

3 Meeting House Lane
Brighton, BN1 1HB
T: 01273 326 080

CHOCCYWOCCYDOODAH

27 Middle Street
Brighton, BN1 1AL
T: 01273 732 232
www.choccywoccydoodah.com

The Mock Turtle Tea Shop
4 Pool Valley
Brighton, BN1 1NJ
T: 01273 327 380

West Brighton & Hove

Beach House Café
21 Kings Road Arches
Brighton, BN1 2LN
T: 08721 486 446

Koba Café
135 Western Road
Brighton, BN3 4FF
T: 01273 720 059

Foodee...licious
75-76 Western Road
Hove, BN3 2JQ
T: 01273 727 909
www.foodee-licious.com

La Fourchette Pâtisserie
42 Church Road
Hove, BN3 2FN
T: 01273 722 556
www.lafourchette.co.uk

9BAR

118 Church Road
Hove, BN3 2EA
T: 01273 721 838
www.9bar.co.uk

MARROCCOS

8 King's Esplanade
Hove, BN3 2WA
T: 01273 203 764
www.marroccos-restaurant.co.uk

CAFFÈ BAR ITALIA DI NAPOLI

24 George Street
Hove, BN3 3YB

HOVE PARK CAFÉ

Hove Park
Hove, BN3 7BF
T: 01273 727 003

DRURY COFFEE & TEA

12-16 Richardson Road
Hove, BN3 5RB
T: 01273 888 600
www.drurysouthern.co.uk

THANKS

Andrew, Selina, Veronika and Fergus at Taylor St.

Taras, Ame and Adam at Coffee@33

Vincent, Thierry and Eddie at Mange Tout

Harry and John at Farm

Laura And Sam at Cream Tea

Tim and Simone at Redroaster

Rick, Matt, Chloe and Ruth at Ground

Sean at Frankie's Grinder

Stephane, Daniel, Caroline and Aurelie at Tic Toc

Richard, Steve, Harry, Rob and Ashley at Marwood

Alan, Brad, Sascha, Tony and Gilda at Small Batch

Alex and Emma at i gigi

Glenda and Sarah-Louise at Ethel's Kitchen

Melody and Alyssa at Treacle & Co.

Also a big thank you to Mr. Smith at the Workshop, B.P. Evans, Susan and Robin Sykes, Jackie and Victor, Meg, Rachael, Sayeeda, Matt Barker, Marc and Arash, Daniel Weller, Ben Adamo, Eleonora d'Ambrosio, James Dean White, Dominic Vacher at Four Corners Print and to Brighton & Hove City Council.

For news and updates on the cafés of
· Brighton & Hove please visit

www.independentcafes.co.uk